I0413323

This book is dedicated to my family and friends. You know who you are.

Hope and Change

That season seemed so long ago, like a precious dream that swept us off our feet, we were lifted to historical heights and taken to unprecedented territory by this idea of hope that was foreign in our lives. By then all hope had been crushed. Jobs were lost, businesses gone; empty storefronts, vacant lots, and lost souls created inner-city ghost towns amidst unrelenting poverty. Children were being murdered, husbands jailed and communities destroyed, leaving gaping holes where humanity once lived.

Change came along like a cool breeze on a hot summer day; it had its way with our hearts, and we were thrilled to be taken so abruptly. Like a star landing in the *hood* we examined it from afar, keeping our distance for fear of being burned again. We were perplexed by its simplicity and thrilled by its potential, yet wary of its promise.

Hope took flight on a cold February morning in 2007. We were skeptical. Others had promised change and not delivered; stars often shined, and faded. This one didn't. It got brighter, so bright we had to shield our souls from its poignant rays. We weren't use to stars landing in our midst and shining so brilliantly. There had been brighter stars; politicians, musicians, actors, athletes, but none had swept us off our feet with such elegance and grace. Our imaginations were lifted by this breath of fresh air. The American dream was placed in our sightlines and we recognized its tangibility. We inhaled deeply, taking in increments of hope while change stirred quietly in the distance. There was suddenly a light at the end of the tunnel, a glimmer of hope that might lead us all to the Promised Land. And the bottom was so painfully crowded we all needed some relief. Before this light shined on us there was no reason to hope; no one was willing to lend a helping hand, or reach down and lift poor people onto the American platform.

Of course we wanted change. If anyone needed inspiration it

was those living at the bottom. America's soul was dying, and the poor needed emergency surgery to repair a human spirit destroyed by the rich and powerful. Maybe this guy had the skills to perform such a complex procedure? In spite of our skepticism - our inability to dream any bigger than our faith could sustain us - hope was on the horizon. Everyone felt it. We had seen glimpses before, but none were like this one. He had the whole package; young, smart, decent, not to mention his confidence. He seemed to believe in the American Dream like no one before him. Then we heard him speak. Some of us had heard him before but nothing like this time, when all the stars had finally aligned. Poignant, charismatic, funny, and with a table spoon of "ism" that didn't come across as being "too" black; too black would have been a deal breaker in 2008. His blackness paralyzed opponents and enthralled a nation. "Black" and "President" combined into a monumental, euphoric moment which lasted for months. Each speech, each gathering of ten, fifteen, and twenty thousand Americans packing arenas all across the nation and singing his praises meant that dream might someday become reality.

He didn't just have "ism", he also had "game." He raised more money and was smarter than all his opponents. History was in the making and we were all participants. We agreed overwhelmingly; America's future was bright again. We had found our shining star. Martin, J.F.K. and Bobby were gunned down halfway up the mountain, maybe this one would carry us all the way to the top. This one was a keeper. He would lead every American to the promised land, and the promised land sounded a whole lot better than the hell we were feeling at the time. He was our knight in shining armor, and we would follow him anywhere. That's the thing about fairytales; we want them to be true, but they're never quite what they seem.

•

When hope fizzles into pain, we become unhinged; rage simmers, and murder and mayhem explode between the divided lines of ghetto walls and the American Dream. Poor people live in that incorrigible space where hope has been left to die. If we don't bear witness to American hypocrisy soon, we will be permanently blinded. There are no great men; there are inspiring individuals with brilliant ideas. If we can push the bullshit aside maybe we can get together and work this thing out, and our potential might finally blossom into the American Dream.

•

If anyone could change the downward trajectory of poor inner-city people, it was Barrack Obama. So charming. So brilliant. Yes, he was our knight in shining armor and in many ways he still is. Becoming America's first Black President was no small feat. He promised to rebuild America from the ground up. Under his guidance poor people would mix with the mainstream and that long awaited dream of equality would finally be realized. Wall Street would accept a few less billion for the betterment of those struggling at the bottom. Mixing fair mindedness with governmental intervention, poor people would join America's mainstream for the first time in this nation's history.

After the election, after the inauguration, after the republican's recovered from their thorough ass whuppin', after the most consequential Presidential election of our lifetime had settled into reality, our high slowly dissipated. Shortly after George W. Bush was booed off the main stage the recession of 2008-9 pummeled poor people into a "depression." (Please! Poor people were in a recession long before the shit hit the fan). Suddenly, that job you'd worked more than twenty years was at risk. The career you'd built was on the line and the banks were threatening to kick you out of your home. Food stamps were siphoned to help fill holes in America's financial structure, but patch one hole and another bust wide open. Poverty trickled into the mainstream as lines at the welfare office grew longer. Those once working nine to five now waited in a line two blocks long outside the public aide office, alongside a single mother of five who has been in that line for ten years, carrying a burden dropped on her by generations of poverty. America has always shitted on her, now that shit has piled up and threatens to take her under.

Long lines outside unemployment offices, welfare offices, Social Security offices, churches, soup kitchens, the Salvation Army, waiting on crumbs, became a theme sung poignantly by the poorest of the poor. Depression equaled devastation. Craters of hopelessness erupted and the ashes landed in the hood, where they now simmer along the American bottom. This is when heroes should rise to the surface of the public sphere. Where are local and national heroes willing to fight for poor people? Where is evidence of heroism beyond speeches and empty promises delivered by politicians? Political representatives have no answers to our problems so they hide in places where the poor can't find them. Republicans aren't hiding; they've stated their intentions loud and clear and without reservation. Instead of working with the President to try and stabilize America's weakened foundation, their sole aim was making sure Barrack Obama was a one term president. Thankfully, they failed miserably.

While campaigning for the presidency Barrack Obama promised to rebuild America from the ground up. Is it his fault Republicans have kept him from reaching all the way to the bottom in the rebuilding process? He expected bipartisanship; reach across the aisle and lets work out our differences. He was naïve. Black and Hispanic children die violent deaths in America's inner-cities every single day. The lives of our children are being cut short because of poverty, plain and simple. Generations are being obliterated, but the

4

republicans have yanked the President back whenever he's tried to implement change. *Less Government!* They shout. *None of your socialist bullshit Obama! We don't care how many people are suffering or how many poor children are dying! They don't fit in our American portrait!* He said it would take time. *Change won't happen overnight,* he said. It hasn't, not in ways we had imagined. Poor people expected some positive change by now. After electing our first Black President we expected America to unite, finally living up to our potential as a nation of the people and for the people. We were naïve. Under his administration race, color, and creed would be discarded and public servants would finally be measured by their deeds. How have they served their constituents? Most have failed. Politicians grow phat posing as public servants. It's time we hold them accountable for their non-action, and the collateral damage they've left behind with a solution to be named later.

Poor People

Poor people move to a beat separate from the mainstream. That bluesy, funky, folksy, hip-hop beat pushes us forward regardless of painful circumstances. The lives of the poor are in the line of fire every single day. *Don't miss a beat, don't stray to far off the beaten path 'cause you might not get straight again. Don't hit that pipe even once or you won't get back on track. Don't flip them rocks and blows for fast money 'cause you'll get caught speeding, and jail and prison will become permanent fixtures in your life.*

Many have strayed because there've been so few opportunities for success. We scavenge for the crumbs thrown at us from America's table of plenty. We are thankful for what we get because at the bottom you survive by any means necessary. American necessity is determined by the bottom line. If the poor ever attained qualitative values through social and economic rehabilitation America's profit margin would lessen, black and brown fathers would be freed from prison, and the shackles from petty drug convictions would finally be loosed from their souls. If America's poor were socially rehabilitated parents would no longer be strung out on rocks and blows, the *War on Drugs* would be thirty billion dollars cheaper, and children would no longer be senselessly murdered in the streets.

•

Poor people are united beneath an umbrella of poverty; background doesn't matter. We help each other; we feed each other and love one another, but America's post racial rhetoric has never moved beyond words. The poor have found ways of transcending racism; the "light" or "dark" complexion of one's skin has surpassed the almighty color line. When you're poor the intonation of one's voice is no longer profiled as "other worldly". Race has been subtracted from the equation. A black woman stripped bare is the same as a Hispanic, Indian or White woman stripped to the bone. At the bottom being dirt poor is our common thread. The American bottom is the one place where humanity has prevailed. If those at the top practiced this kind of unity, if they had enough perspective to take a closer look inside America's core, they might learn a few things about racialism from those who have already kicked that shit to the curb.

.

The *Hood* represents that wretched place where the poor reside in squalor. The chronically homeless and mentally ill have been pummeled by enemy weaponry from the very beginning; bombs exploded and shots were fired long before we knew what hit us. We have been barraged by attacks from our oppressor for so long trauma has become our baseline. We are war torn. Blood flows aimlessly through inner-city streets but we still haven't realized that we're under attack. This is ass backwards. Unfortunately, this has become the American way.

.

Social services have been snatched away without replacement; food stamps have been cut (and face further cuts) and our young men are imprisoned at alarming rates. We must fight against this! Violence has escalated in inner-cities because those with no money and few resources are seized by desperation. The poor turn to addiction and crime for purposes of survival, and as coping mechanisms. We should demand that the local, state and the federal government fund programs that will inspire our youth generation, and provide respite from unrelenting poverty.

Republican governors have stripped unions of their bargaining rights, and they've implemented laws that will make it harder for poor people to vote. Republican lawmakers want to do away with the Department of Education while black and Hispanic men fill more jails and prisons than they do colleges and universities. We must fight against this! Their plan for growth? Tax breaks for billionaires and building more prisons as a means of supplying American jobs. Enough with the plantation politics. Less education and more prisons doesn't add up to change we can believe in. We must fight this!

•

Giving tax breaks to billionaires is illogical, but logic has been subtracted from America's political equation. Being poor means we must fight for bigger government! If we don't our lives will worsen before they get better. Without governmental intervention poor people will suffer irreparable mental and physical damage that will be passed down through the generations, and will threaten our existence. Once the Republicans, a delusional Congress, and a compromised Supreme Court finish taking away the few rations we depend on for survival, more of us will be locked in jails, and even more will be dead.

•

No one has to tell you that you're poor; you know it because you feel it everyday. When there's no money for food or to pay the bills hopelessness creeps upon you like a ticking bomb waiting to explode. It seems unfair that the poor should suffer for mistakes made by those who aren't suffering. It is our job to make them care. Poor people believe in traditional American values just like everyone else, but we suffer from profound naivety. Our circumstances are dire, yet we believe humanity will someday prevail. It should. Unfortunately those making America's critical decisions aren't humanitarians; they are greedy congressmen and billionaires. The kindest heart is often the first to be obliterated; the soft spoken are rarely heard. The Native American should have killed every one of those pilgrims who landed on Plymouth Rock; fathers, mothers, children should have all been killed. Instead, the Native American trusted these white people, genocide was committed against them, and they were wiped off the face of the earth. When the Portuguese arrived on African soil we should have killed them

8

before they got off the boat. Instead, black people were sold into slavery by our own people.

How can so few white people rule so many Black people? Malcolm X once asked. Slaves outnumbered their "so-called" masters by great numbers. Instead of just Denmark Vesey and Nat Turner there should have been a massive revolt across the south by all slaves to overthrow an inhumane regime conveniently been left in place by our founding fathers. We should have forced them to accept us as human beings in this foreign land. Instead, both Denmark and Nat's revolts were quashed. Slavery continued. Slavery remains.

Principles of divide and conquer were implemented hundreds of years ago just as they are today. Black men fill jail and prison cells because we've been taught to hate ourselves; we were taught to hate the color of our skin, the coarseness of our hair and the harshness of our condition. Poor blacks are convinced that we belong on the bottom and on the bottom, killing each other, is where we languish. We need to be lifted and our youth need to be inspired, but there is no one offering an encouraging voice, or lending a helping hand.

•

How do poor people recover from overwhelming circumstances? Bit by bit, and step by step; just do a little better than you did yesterday and don't expect recovery to be like fireworks going off in the sky. Remove those blinders so you can clearly see what's going on around you. You know your son is selling drugs. You know your nephew is in a gang and deep down you know why. Too many young men have been thrust into the role of manhood without preparation, and gangs offer a distorted version of the manhood they crave. Dad is gone, or he's never been around and they feel a duty to provide for their families. Flipping rocks and blows is the only job available when you're uneducated, untrained and coming from up off the block. They won't do better until we do better. They

9

won't thrive until we get up off our hands and knees and fight for their lives, and our own, and the generations that will follow.

•

Sometimes you have to scrap what hasn't worked and start over, the poor have fallen just that far. Broken generations don't heal with time; lives don't gradually get better unless the course of those lives are redirected toward positive solutions. Qualitative counseling and treatment for various afflictions affecting individuals, families, and communities must be enhanced, or the lives of poor people will worsen before they get better.

•

Trauma is generational. *My mama beating me teaches me to beat my child. In some cases daddy raping me teaches me, subconsciously, to rape my little cousin.* Pain perpetuates pain, addiction perpetuates addiction, and abandonment perpetuates abandonment. We lead our lives according to how we've been taught by parents, family, friends, peers, and both the *inner* and *outer* circles of society.

•

The *inner circle* includes the family household. In the "hood" this typically means a single mother raising two or three children. The father's of these children are either not around or unaccountable, incarcerated, or such an abusive presence in the household that mother and children are better off with him gone. Love is still prevalent in these households. Black and Hispanic mothers love their children just as much as white mothers, but its expression has been quashed and muted by fear and lack of expectation.

•

Inner-city neighborhoods are defined by "clusters." That sect of Black men who hung out and drank on street corners still exist. The difference between then and now? These men were

10

once employed at the steel mill, bakery or at some factory. They were the head of their house holds. When mother called for dinner they were seated at the head of the table, blessing their food and the lives of their families.

In the last thirty years this sect of Black and Hispanic men have joined the ranks of the unemployed. Their earning potential has been removed from the community. More importantly, their financial stability and presence has been stripped from the family equation. Black and Hispanic men between the ages of thirty and forty have been removed from our communities at such a high volume, the fallout feels like a tornado has blown through our lives, and wiped them away. These men either never returned once they climbed over ghetto walls - going away to college, finding a good job and moving into a safer, more affluent community - or they've been swallowed into that systematic revolving door of the jail and prison system. Many have lost all hope and succumbed to drugs, or are homeless and suffering from an undiagnosed mental illness. The only semblance of manhood left in the "hood" are adolescent drug dealers and gang members; they have become a strong, intimidating male presence. They influence our children and dictate the mood of our communities. When the goal of a fourteen year old on any given day is survival, gangs offer protection, and a "phantom love" these kids don't get at home. Most are willing to pay the severe price of gang participation. There is no *Brady Bunch* or *Cosby Show* behind ghetto walls; no examples of architects, lawyers, doctors, or businessmen going to and from work. Most twenty and thirty year olds don't know how to be better parents - better men or women - because they've never had qualitative examples to teach them. I know "right" from "wrong" because my mother "taught" me instead of "beating" me. Giving birth doesn't mean you instinctively develop proper nurturing skills. Many of our young parents need as much guidance as the children they're bringing into this world; some need to heal from the pain inflicted and passed down through the generations.

•

Critical circumstances won't change overnight; healing a heart wounded at birth won't happen in a few days. Patience with yourself and others is your strongest weapon. The slightest progress can add up to huge gains. Remember this. Love is stronger than hate. Kindness is more powerful than cruelty. Humanity is more potent than the inhumane.

Poor Black People

Black love for our President is laced with pain, pride, and passion born from years of humiliation and degradation as residents, if not always equal citizens of these United States. As we watch him guide this country with such a delicate stroke, many of us know the road he took to get there; the backs he climbed and the history that carried him along with pride and passion, and against all odds. Reaching that presidential podium and speaking truth to light was a monumental achievement. Many of us have worked hard and dreamed big just like him; we've suffered the way he has suffered because our black skin has been treated like a stain on that beautiful American flag. We now wear that stain like a medal of honor. One of us made it to the mountain top. One of us was strong enough, smart enough, and savvy enough to endure that grueling path from behind "ghetto" walls and earn this nations highest seat. Ninety-nine percent of black Americans will love him no matter what he does. *Just be President, that's enough.* The problem? We need more than what's been offered so far, and we need it now; tomorrow will be too late. If we don't find respite soon many more will die, and our future will dissipate before our very eyes. Their bones will be buried in the ground. Again and again, we will have failed them before they can reach their potential.

•

Middle class American's, the "so-called" ninety-nine percent, protest through occupation and nonviolent resistance. Gays have fought and won the repeal of "Don't Ask, Don't Tell." In New York and other states they've won the right to legally marry. Gay Americans are living proof that if you fight hard enough you can win. Black people are fighting, but we're fighting each other. White people once hung black folk from trees as *Strange Fruit*. Billie Holiday transformed the severity of that pain into beauty, through song.

Southern trees, bearing a strange fruit, blood on the leaves, and blood at the root. Black bodies swingin' in the southern

breeze. Strange fruit hangin' from the poplar trees.
Black people remain a strange fruit rotting on American soil.
Blood drips from our souls and flows along the curbs of
inner city streets all cross America. Since the abolishment of
slavery America hasn't known what to do with us. During
reconstruction, *she* terrorized us, angry that freedom had been
given to those deemed "three-fifths" human being. We endured.
She segregated us; better to keep "niggers" confined in their
own squalor than offer them humanity. We endured. The Civil
Rights movement chipped away at ghetto walls, bit by bit. The
Nation of Islam and the Black Panthers of the sixties showed
America there were still Black folk around who didn't mind
fighting the way America liked to fight. Because these black folk
were fearless and brave, big chunks were blasted from ghetto
walls. This allowed a few of us to escape the hood and make it
to the other side. The sixties combined "hope" and "change"
into a revolution of monumental proportions. How do you stop
a revolution? You cut off its head. Medgar Evers was
assassinated at the doorstep of his Mississippi home. John F.
Kennedy was assassinated in Dallas. Malcolm X at the Audubon
ballroom in New York. Dr. King at the Lorraine Hotel in
Memphis in the midst of organizing the "poor people's
campaign." Bobby was killed in California ... and the beat goes
on.

•

The masses of poor black people have felt only humiliation as
residents of America. We've been treated like animals rather
than human beings. Yes, our children kill each other, but it is
America who taught us how to put a gun to our own heads, as if
they were at fault for our miserable condition. America then
taught us how to pull the trigger. We've been taught how to
rape our children the way slave masters once raped our
mothers and daughters, because certain behavior is engrained
in the soul. America has imprisoned our young fathers like

14

slaves ... as if hundreds of years of oppression wasn't a high enough price to pay for being black in a nation where "white" is the only thing "right." America taught us how to hate ourselves more than we hate our oppressor. She has shown poor black people absolutely no love, all the while providing ample means for self-destruction. Rocks and blows echo chaotically from behind ghetto walls; just pick your poison because it's readily available. America has stolen whatever love we've managed to scrape from our own ruins. What's left for poor black people to cling to? If we don't stand up and fight sooner than later it will be too late. Where is our outrage? Why haven't we forced our way onto the main stage and demanded that our grievances be heard? Poor people are the American majority, but we're so politically quiet one could hear a pin drop in our presence.

•

Millionaires are the beneficiaries of unfair tax policies that add more bricks to ghetto walls. Make no mistake about it, if you're poor republicans want you snuffed out. You! The poorest of the poor! They don't care about your plight. That black man who was running for the 2012 republican Presidential nomination said that black people are "brain washed." Not only is he clueless, but he's so far out of touch with his own people he might as well be sitting in Clarence Thomas's lap. Blackness is more than skin tone. Blackness means suffering because you were born black in America, a country that once declared you had no rights which white people should respect. Blackness means humility because we are more than willing to love those who will love us back. Blackness in America means perpetual servitude, although our undeserved debt has been paid tenfold. Blackness means adversity. We were brought here in a storm and through dangerous, reckless seas. Here in America and battling that very same storm is where we languish. Blackness is a stain because America never lets you forget the color of your skin. You pay a price for being

15

black every second of every minute of every day. We have all paid a price. Many of our children have paid our portion with their lives. We are paid in deep. It's time we withdrew some equity from the sweat, pain, and tears we've been paying out to America for hundreds of years.

•

Black fathers have filled jails and prisons since the abolishment of slavery. For these men "freedom" is just a word. Most have been convicted of drug related crimes, yet we've done little to help lift these brothers from their jail and prison infected lives. Once released from downstate prisons or Cook County jail they return to their families, and our communities, more bitter and traumatized than before their incarceration. Pain begets pain and our children - our communities - suffer tremendous consequences. There is little aftercare for ex-felons outside of a thinly veiled probation or parole system. They've had hope ripped from their souls. A man can't maintain a solid family structure if they're caught up in crime and addiction. Do they need jobs? Of course they do, but it's impossible to sustain gainful employment because of drug related felonies. Most have never been given the proper tools to succeed. Recovery isn't magical. It is a hurtful, painstaking process. We won't move forward or gain any ground until we heal our suffering wounds. Our black men won't get up off their hands and knees until we lift them up. Lift them, and give them something to cling to. Offer them strength, love, and forgiveness, and watch them change the world.

The Politico and the Media

Poor people live daily, impoverished lives. The blood of our children flows through the streets. The national, liberal media has not yet arrived on the scene. They can do better. I remain hopeful that they will.

No one is running to your rescue because you haven't let them know you're at risk. We have to kick our congressmen's door down and let them know how badly their constituents are hurting. Take them to task for talking in circles while providing absolutely no leadership. Call them out for their dead silence in your greatest hour of need. Your life is on the line but these representatives are nowhere on the scene. We need our elected officials to be lions. If not, get the hell out the way so we can elect people who know how to fight, tooth and nail, the way this "new" America likes to fight; with votes instead of ropes and trees.

Instead of allowing politicians and pundits to obliterate the poor, lets start an inclusive conversation amongst ourselves and try solving our own problems. Stop letting politicians use your voice as if it were their own. They don't represent you; they represent the rich. In the next election demote their asses. Grab them by the collar and drag them to the bottom so they can feel some of the hell you've been living everyday in this land of the free and home of the brave.

•

At best, our space on the American platform is unsteady. Abortion rights activists have a place. Islamist and Tea Partiers are right there in the front row. Even that storefront preacher who threatened to burn the Koran on the anniversary of 911 found a space on that platform, until he was kicked off. The mentally ill remain on the fringe. Black people are locked behind ghetto walls. The homeless are invisible in plain sight. Americans dying without dignity should be a travesty. When children are murdered senselessly there should be an outcry unleashed so loud it could be heard from every corner of this nation. Here at the bottom, outrage has been weakened by poverty. The national, liberal media has not yet arrived on the scene.

17

•

Political speak doesn't pay the bills. Empty promises won't pay the rent and mortgage. Backroom deals don't buy clothes for our children. Campaign promises won't feed our families. Open your eyes! Stop being blinded by campaign promises that never see the light of day. It's time we start treating politicians like the public servants they are. That's right, they work for us and we should evaluate them accordingly. Contrasting the lackluster effort put forth by politicians against our daily pain puts us in a perfect position to measure their worth. Big city councilmen and other state and federal officials earn six figure salaries. Has "he" or "she" come up with any innovative ideas to enhance the quality of your community? Have they added anything of value? Or have they stood idly by while your livelihood has played the role of sacrificial lamb? Do you even know their names? Think about it. You walk in that voting booth and check off a name on a ballot, but do you know anything about these politicians campaigning to represent you? That's like hiring a plumber to fix your sink or an accountant to do your taxes without knowing their qualifications, because you haven't interviewed them; you haven't reviewed their resume. More importantly, you haven't interviewed others who might be better qualified, as human beings instead of politicians. That name you mark on that ballot, that invisible person you've hired to advocate for you, is a wasted vote. Our vote is worth its weight in gold. When we're neglectful and don't do our homework we make things harder on ourselves. In the next election we must elect public officials who can add corporeal value to our lives. If we don't our vote depreciates. We can only be considered "three-fifths" human being if we allow our vote to be devalued.

•

Do we know the job description of our elected officials? And how do those responsibilities impact our lives? Do they

18

promote legislation that adversely effects our family, friends, and communities? Do they vote in line with the mayor or governor just to gain political favor? Or do they fight tooth and nail for you, their constituents? Look out your front window. The answer is on the streets. We must ask ourselves these critical questions. Do politicians truly have our best interest at heart? And if the former is true, if they've done more harm than good, do we really want them working for us? When firing season is upon us don't we have a right to fire that public servant who has served us miserably? If they're asked to address a community concern and that request is ignored, don't we have the right, as Americans, to go in that voting booth and fire their asses? Yes we do. *And yes we can!*

I'm sure there are some elected officials out here doing the job we've hired them to do. At the very least, I am hopeful. The problem is that we don't know for sure. We need big thinkers representing us; folks who can think "way" outside the box when the nation is strapped for money and new ideas. I'd be willing to bet you are one of those big thinkers; average Joe or Tina waiting in the wings to change the world, or at the very least, impact your community.

●

We must take our elected officials to task and demand that they tell us why our lives are so painful. Ask them why our children are being murdered and no one is doing anything to stop this! Confront your Congressman and ask them why the cold-blooded murder of black and Hispanic children hasn't created a *"state of emergency!"* instead of dismissive blurbs on the evenings news. When firing season (election day) arrives, don't settle for generic, useless rhetoric meant to pacify us. We know times are hard, we feel it everyday. Of course we know the nation is strapped for money; tell us something we don't know but we insist that you tell us the truth. If you lie we will come to your office and kick your door down in search

19

of the honesty we deserve! Tell us why monies are spent so disproportionately in upscale neighborhoods than in inner city communities? Why has Chicago's south side been stereotyped so violently with nothing being done to combat these atrocities? Murder and mayhem in the "hood" is real on many levels, but we must to take a closer look at the problem to understand the full caption of what's being presented on the evening news. We should demand that our elected officials take a closer look, and take decisive action in combating the carnage that ravishes poor communities. We pay them. They should earn that "phat" paycheck deposited in their bank accounts each month. Why should they get paid while you're struggling to survive and fighting to keep your family afloat? It's their job to be your advocate. They are coming up way short.

•

Violence has pulverized poor communities all across America. Those hiding behind political positions are rarely around to feel the aftermath of inner city pain, but are in front of cameras dissecting violence well after the shit has hit the fan. Crisis happens in the moment. The crushing, demoralizing impact violence brings to families and friends is paralyzing. If public officials were to feel some of that pain, personally, if they ever held a six year old in their arms as they bled to death from a gunshot wound, their critiques might be different. If they felt the pain that poverty brings to families, maybe they'd bring more answers to the table than rhetoric.

•

Poor people have been excluded from the American conversation. The media, pundits, lobbyist, and politicians have all asserted that a so-called "conversation" must take place before America can dig herself out of the economic, racially divisive hell we're in right now. I don't know about you, but I haven't heard anything said worthwhile: nothing that deals with issues concerning you and I. Our fate is left to those who barely know we exist. We reject this philosophy of top down decision making! When the voices of America's most vulnerable citizens are silenced, it's time to flip the script. Rise Up! Revolt! Revolutionize your mind and you might revolutionize a nation and help quash political corruption that has kept America's foot on your throat for far too long.

Perhaps complacency has blinded the liberal media to the poor people's plight. Maybe the rap on them is true: just a bunch of "do-gooders" who address daily, topical issues. They can help fix this. They can expose genocide being committed against poor people in the United States of America just as their predecessors did in the sixties. During the Civil Rights Movement the media thrust American atrocities into the mainstream. In many respects they risked their lives covering crimes committed against poor, southern blacks. Racist segregationist were violent and the media wasn't immune to that violence. They traveled to the south and faced their fears while exposing American carnage. MSNBC, CNN, CBS and other media outlets were present throughout the Arab spring; many put their lives on the line while covering revolution erupting in other countries. What about the bloodshed, poverty, and hopelessness destroying American lives right outside their backdoors? Why haven't they reached behind ghetto walls and shined their national spotlight on genocide being committed on American soil? Why haven't they gone to the American bottom and stood side by side with those who are hurting the most, the same way they stood with the Egyptians? Why haven't they talked to the people, the poor people, to better understand their plight, and descent?

In 2014, and beyond, they can help give voice to those who barely have the strength to whisper. Trauma cripples the soul. Being beaten subtracts ones ability to voice outrage, and distress has a way of silencing those suffering the worst. We depend on others to speak for those of us who can no longer speak for ourselves.

When hurricane Katrina devastated New Orleans the media coverage was 24/7. When an earthquake pummeled Haiti ordinary Americans reached out with kindness and empathy that matched the pain of Haiti's suffering people. What about those suffering right outside the NBC and Fox News buildings? What about the homeless right outside the White House? They aren't invisible. You see them but you choose to ignore them. I will interpret the credibility of your silence. You have done nothing! Excluding the poor from the American conversation is unjust. Refusing to report on poverty's source is negligent, especially when it lives in plain sight. You can do better. I remain hopeful that you will.

Stop Killing Kids

Slavery has trickled down through the generations. Some will refute this. They say get over it; slavery is old news that ended a hundred and fifty years ago, but its resin remains in plain sight. Teenage black boys clustered on street corners are the collateral damage left over from slavery. After school they should be playing sports or involved in the arts, but policies based on Reaganomics have wiped these programs out. Reaganomics brought ready rock into the hood and turned their parents into crack heads; parents then gave their love to the streets instead of their children. This was a powerful blow to the hearts of our youth. Now they look into the eyes of loveless parents, then turn to the streets in search of the parental love they've lost so many years ago.

•

Trauma has many weapons, but prison is the most potent. The shackles of modern day slavery have been clamped onto the souls of our children and dismantled their core values. America grabs our youth and bashes their souls against ghetto walls. They are backed into dark corners the day they are born. They learn to fight for their lives before they are weaned off the bottle.

•

Why do our children cluster outside of liquor stores and fast food joints, where both victim and prey become interchangeable? I'll tell you. We have placed them there. Why do they dress in opposing fashion to the mainstream, yet their fashion often defines the *"look"* of the world? Why does their swagger represent danger? Perhaps danger has been thrust on them, and that swagger is armor worn as protective gear, keeping them safe from a nation that has always despised them. Their demeanor is fearsome and writhed in pain, yet distinguishable and independent and worn with a sense of freedom. Their language is laced with rhyme and reason twisted into beautiful lyrics, but we rarely hear them

23

when they speak. Their dreams simmer beneath the public sphere. Their words are often articulated profanely, but our youth own their independence, which is more than I can say for the rest of us; the "so-called" responsible faction. They refuse to change when asked to conform. They long to be heard, but their voices are rejected by the mainstream. Some defy the odds; others die defending their independence.

•

What is the magic of guns, drugs and violence that has our kids spellbound and killing each other at such alarming rates? I'll tell you. Power! The weight of cold steel makes them strong when poverty has weakened them. Pulling that trigger makes them judge and jury. Pinned up rage from years of trauma is released in an instant, punishing anyone who happens to be at the wrong place at the wrong time. The question? How is a five year old at the wrong place at the wrong time when they're walking home from school? How is a nine year old at the wrong place at the wrong time when they're jumping rope in front of their home? How is a thirteen year old at the wrong place at the wrong time when they're playing basketball at the park? I'll tell you. America has systematically failed to protect poor children. Instead of removing bricks of poverty and allowing rays of hope to shine through, more have been added, blocking whatever potential that might seep through the cracks. Historically, they've had very little to depend on. Poor kids have never been offered a quality education, which was once the building block solidifying America's future. No more after school programs keeping that idle mind away from the devils prowling eye. No more grown men on the scene showing them a pathway to manhood, because black men have been chained, shackled, and locked away in prisons. No more fathers protecting their daughters from the wolves who circle them and wait for just the right moment to pounce. They rape, punish, and impregnate our daughters and move on to the next fourteen or fifteen year old girl whose vulnerability is worn on her sleeve. Their future is destroyed before it begins. Destruction breeds destruction, and only the strong survive. The weak are devoured.

•

TYRONE enters. He is in his late teens and dressed in jeans and a sweater. He stops in his tracks when he sees KENNY standing near his younger brother, Michael.

TYRONE
(approaching them cautiously)
What are you doing here?

KENNY
(shrugging)
I ... I was invited.

TYRONE
Aint nobody bothered you, Kenny. Me and my family are just trying to make it from day to day. We don't need your kind of trouble around here.

MICHAEL
Kenny didn't come here to start trouble. I brought him here. He's Anton's big brother.

TYRONE
Why couldn't you stay with your mama?

KENNY
(pause)
I guess 'cause I messed up too bad. Mama said she didn't want me in her house no more.

25

TYRONE

I can understand that. You aint nothin' but trouble.

KENNY

I did a lot of bad things. I've already accepted that part.
(pause)
I'm still tryin' to find a way to live with all the bad stuff I've done.
(pause)
That's the hard part.

TYRONE
(seething)
I hope you never find any peace. I hope it eats you up inside for the rest of your life.

MICHAEL

Come on Tyrone. He admitted the things he did was wrong. Everybody deserves a second chance.

TYRONE

Some people don't deserve a second chance, Michael. Some of the things he did are unforgivable. He deserves to be in prison. He just never got caught.

KENNY
(barely remorseful)
Man, I don't even remember most of that stuff. When shit went down I was always high or drunk or sumpin'. I know I shot a lot of people and I probably even killed some, but I don't remember none of it. I can't see their faces because they wasn't even real people to me.

26

TYRONE

You killed a lot of people. You killed a lot of my friends.
(simmering)
You killed my girlfriend.

LIGHTS DIM. A Photograph of TYRONE'S girlfriend, LINDA, flashes against the back wall.

TYRONE

Linda wasn't doin' nothin' wrong.. She was just standin' outside that corner store after buying some bleach for her mother. You and yo niggas rolled up and saw a crowd of people and just started blastin'.
(pause)
She wasn't but sixteen years old. She lived three more days after she was shot. She whispered in my ear who shot her. She said she looked her killer right in the eye. Say she looked at him, pleading for him not to kill her, but he did it anyway.
(looking right at him)
It was you.

KENNY

(remorseful)
I don't ... know what to say to that.
(shrugging)
I would say I'm sorry but it really wouldn't mean much. If I could take it back I would but I caint. I'm gonna have to live with what I done the rest of my life. Aint nothin' I can do to change that part.

TYRONE

(infuriated)
You could turn yourself into the police. You can be accountable for your actions.

KENNY

I could. I've thought about that. But I'd have to remember what I did, people and places, in order to understand why I'm going to prison. And I just don't remember. Bits and pieces here and there don't add up to a complete picture.

TYRONE removes pictures from his coat pocket; holding them with a tight grip, The pictures flash against the back wall in repetition.

TYRONE

You want proof, Kenny? I got proof for you right here.

He takes one of the pictures and thrust it toward him; it is a school picture of his girlfriend smiling from ear to ear. Each of LINDA'S pictures flash against a wall UPSTAGE.

TYRONE

This is Linda. This is her eighth grade picture. She was happy then. Can you see it? She was looking forward to going on her eighth grade trip to Washington D.C.
    (thrusting another picture toward him)
This is her at the Capital. Do you see how beautiful she is? You can look in her eyes and see how much hope she had for the future.

KENNY

    (shunning him)
Come on, yo. I don't want to do this.

TYRONE

    (hovering over him; thrusting another picture
    in his face)
You the one said you couldn't remember. This is her as a

TYRONE
(continued)
freshman in high school. She was a cheerleader. Vice president
of her class. She wanted to be a journalist. She wanted to write
about Aids and famine in Africa. This sixteen year old girl was
thinking about those things when you fools was ridin' around
gettin' high and smokin' blunts.

*KENNY recognizes one of the pictures. A frightened look covers
his face. He takes the picture in his hand and looks at it,
painfully.*

KENNY
I remember this girl.
(looking from the picture to TYRONE)
I didn't know she was your girlfriend, but I remember her. She
was the prettiest girl in the neighborhood.

TYRONE
(thrusting pictures of LINDA at him
in repetition)
This is her singing in the school choir. This is her on the
national debate team. This is her playing for the volleyball city
championship. This is she and I in the park. This is us on
Christmas morning, on prom, my high school graduation ...

He grasp a picture firmly in his hands, looking at it closely.

TYRONE
This is her after you shot her in the face. There were bullet
fragments in her hands because she was trying to fight them off.
This is her on the ground. This is the blood streaming down the
sidewalk. This is her mother screaming and crying outside the
emergency room. This is her sister collapsing in her mothers

TYRONE

(continued)
arms. This is the pain, the heartache felt from losing such a
special person much too soon.
(looking at him; piercingly; tears
streaming from his eyes)
This was the life of Linda Graves. This is what you stole from
so many people who loved her.

·

Politicize your mind. Don't just start a conversation about our
youth, dictate the message. The language of these young people
is often perplexing to old schoolers like me. The texture of their
words can be crass and offensive, but beauty is often painful to
American senses, and poetry is written to make us "feel." Fond
memories of the seventies and eighties fled without ever saying
goodbye; no kisses or hugs, just gone. Innovative times are
within our midst, but we haven't fully embraced them. Lets
welcome this new generation back into our hearts. Take some
time and get to know them, and how can we ever know them
without a measure of understanding? An olive branch must be
extended. One generation must let the other know they're
welcome home again. We let this happen, not them. We failed
them, they didn't fail us. We have all suffered the consequences.

·

After so much damage has been done we should ask ourselves
why we've stopped loving them? Measured glances aren't
enough; distant reasoning solves nothing. If we don't critique
the potential loss of "this" generation things will
never get better. This time, or maybe next time, they won't
recover.

·

What keeps us from looking at the core problems propelling
these kid's descent into obliteration? Take a closer look, please,
so we can find solutions and remove a few more bricks from

ghetto walls? That mother draped over the coffin of her sixteen year old son is painfully puzzling. He too just happened to be at the wrong place at the wrong time, not because he was in a gang or out selling drugs, but because we thrust him into dangerous places. Because of our failures these kids are always in the line of fire. If we want real solutions we must take a much deeper look at deep seeded problems. Our failure to do so speaks of cowardice. Fear has paralyzed our ability to affect change.

•

The poor need a recovery plan to heal the damage that has trickled down through the generations. If the pathway to recovery is crooked and graveled, how can poor kids ever recover? If the playing field is uneven how will they prosper? And the beat goes on, painful and grinding with elements of pride and beauty laced between the songs of our lives. We tap our feet and clap our hands to that beat; we cry tears that should have run dry years ago. We cling to a single thread of hope that helps us survive each day, but that thread has worn thin, burdened by the weight of poor people being shoved from the cusp of the American Dream. Tonight, more children will die, and that beat will grind slowly, painfully against our hearts. Increments of hope and change are no longer enough; we need the whole thing and we need it now! Tomorrow will be too late! When they leave the corner many go straight to jail. Many more will land in emergency rooms; some will go straight to the trauma unit. As they fade into shock, they might think the flashing lights and blaring sirens are beautiful. On the operating table, clothes and chest ripped open as surgeons hover over them, reality will set in. They will reflect on their mistakes and their mortality. Death will snatch many before their fifteenth birthday They will die alone. Alone, in the wilderness, is where we have left them.

•

LIGHTS UP on gunshot victim lying on a table. A SURGEON

31

has just completed surgery and stands over him. DIM LIGHT above sobbing MOTHER. The SURGEON removes his mask and gloves and approaches her.

MOTHER
(expecting the very worst)
Is my boy going to be okay?

SURGEON
(pause)
No.

MOTHER collapses to her knees. She sobs uncontrollably.

MOTHER
(lifting her hands upward)
Oh my God! No! Not my baby! No God! Don't take him yet!
He was such a good boy!

The SURGEON watches MOTHER with perplexed eyes.

SURGEON
He'll live. With a few months of rehab he'll probably even walk
again.

MOTHER
(standing; barely collecting herself)
Why would you say something like that, then? What kind of
person are you?

SURGEON
You didn't ask me if he would live. You asked if he would be
okay.

32

                    SURGEON
          (pause/continued)
No. He most certainly will not be okay.

                     MOTHER
You knew what I was asking.

                    SURGEON
Being alive and "being okay" are two different things.
          (pause)
Yes. He will live. But no, he will not be okay. If it weren't
unethical I would have just let him die.
          (looking back at the boy on the table)
At this rate, he'll probably do more harm than good for
however
long he lives in this world.
          (pause)
His other wounds are terminal.

                     MOTHER
What other wounds? Are you crazy?

                    SURGEON
I assure you I am quite sane, mam.
          (looking at MOTHER carefully)
How old is your son?

                     MOTHER
          (suspicious)
He's ... he's nineteen. Why do you ask?

                    SURGEON
Do you know how many gunshot wounds your son has in his
body?

MOTHER

I don't see what that has to do with anything?

SURGEON
(pause)
Nine.
(pause)
He's nineteen years old and he has already been shot nine times.

MOTHER

That caint be true.

SURGEON

He has one in his right shoulder.

MOTHER

I don't believe you.

SURGEON

One is in his bicep.

MOTHER
(taken aback)
He told me he hurt his arm at football practice.

SURGEON

He has another one in his stomach.

MOTHER
(covering her mouth: breaking down)
He said he had a bad stomach ache. I wondered ... I wondered why there was so much blood.

SURGEON

There are gunshot wounds in his left thigh and right calf.

MOTHER

(certain of this)

That one was not a gunshot wound. His leg hurt so bad that time he needed crutches.

(pause)

He was a star football player in high school and got all kinds of injuries.

(laughing painfully)

If it aint one thing it's always another.

The SURGEON takes a single step toward mother. She measures him cautiously.

SURGEON

Some of these wounds can be repaired.

(pause)

Others cannot.

MOTHER

(optimistic)

Lets just deal with today, then. Okay?

(smiling nervously)

That's all we've got work with … right?

SURGEON

You ignorance is your greatest crime.

MOTHER

What?

SURGEON

Your child is dying because you are weak. Your inability to
face the truth has mortgaged his future.

MOTHER

You don't even know me, mister. You just a doctor.
(pause)
That don't make you God.

SURGEON

I know you better than you know yourself. Mother's like you
come in here crying over your fallen children as if they have
accidentally landed in dangerous places.

MOTHER
(pressing her hand against her chest)
You sayin' I'm at fault for my son getting shot?

SURGEON
(pause)
Yes. That's exactly what I'm saying. You've done more damage
to your child than any bullet could ever do.

MOTHER

How dare you?

SURGEON

I understand the many complications involved in parenting
while living in poverty. I understand there are things that are
simply out of your control. But I also know there have been
opportunities for you to save him.
(pause)
Yet, you've chosen not to.

MOTHER

Shut up! Just … shut up!

SURGEON

Instead, you have left him in the wilderness for the wolves
to devour. These boys are being eaten alive and no one is doing
anything to stop it. Not you. Not me. Not anyone.
> (pause)

I can patch them up, but I can't fix what has been so tragically
broken inside.
> (pause)

Neither can you.
> (pause)

I guess that's the shame of it all.

•

Our children have been wandering directionless and along
dangerous terrain for far too long. The wolves are eating them
alive. They circle them, study them, and consume them. We
could rescue them but instead we have refused them our loving
embrace. We once hugged and kissed our kids lovingly, then
everything changed. Someone blinked and our lives were
different.

•

Why are we willing to give them away freely when they should
be our most precious gems? We've sold our future and
received little in return; only pain, worry and much more
heartache than we can bear. We've stopped fueling the souls
of our youth who yearn desperately to be inspired by
something, anything they can feel. Young souls need to be fed
with frequency. They are hungry and will consume whatever is
offered. There's been so little good stuff available we've kept it
all for ourselves. We feed our kids garbage; they give it back
tenfold.

•

Why have our children landed on street corners and accepted the dangerous embrace of gangs? America's broken educational system bears some responsibility. Our best and brightest are unable to dissect the critical condition of America's educational climate. Pubic schools in poor neighborhoods are dilapidated. Expectations of success have been placed on the shoulders of these faltering institutions without providing them with the tools to succeed. We have placed educational responsibilities on parents already dodging debris flung at them from ghetto walls. Teachers three years removed from college are incapable of teaching kids with complex problems stimulated from "hood economics." The truth? Opportunities for success have never been offered to poor children. Overcrowded classrooms don't reflect equality. Teachers spend too much time dealing with personal tragedies spilling over from the home rather than focusing on their teaching responsibilities. They are forced to deal with problems with mom and dad when mom and dad were once a stabilizing force that kept the family structure solid. What happens when that structure is weakened by addiction and trauma? It breaks ... and comes crumbling down on the "hood." If dad is locked up in jail or prison we can understand how the crumbling pieces from the family structure end up flipping rocks and blows on street corners. When the position of leader/role model/breadwinner is extracted from that structure the family burden is then placed on the mother. If the family includes five or six kids, some with different fathers, those problems multiply, and the mother eventually weakens and succumbs to poverty. The children are then left to fend for themselves. This is no longer an American possibility. This is reality, and it's created madness and mayhem for all involved.

•

A person won't respect anything if they haven't been shown a pathway to civility. A discourse in the process is missing. Some of these kinks can be repaired. Give a little love and you might get some back. Offer pain and it will be returned tenfold. Confirm that young woman's self worth so she won't believe the lies from wicked men trying to get in her panties. Smile instead of frowning so much; a smile and a teaspoon of laughter are worth their weight in gold, but we don't use them nearly enough. Some will mistake your kindness for something else and try and make it scandalous. These are teachable moments; each one must teach one in order to make our journey a little better, and to give hope to a faltering generation. Some moments are so precious we miss them. We can't afford to miss anymore. Grab them as if they were stars pulled down from the sky. Hold them in your hands and mesh them with your heart, and marvel at their duplicity.

•

Black and Hispanic teenagers have been branded as uncouth. I'm sure they're hurt by these stereotypes, because evil is what some have given back to the world. Yet, they have so much more to offer. Their contribution to the world might be the greatest of all time, but we'll never know because we kill them off instead of building them up. Dad in and out of jail thrust a knife into their souls. Mom's new boyfriend beating and raping them removes huge portions of humanity that were once God given, leaving gaping holes that have never been refilled. Poor education leaves them stagnant, subtracting American potential from their personal equation. Hunger pains, no heat or lights and watching as their younger siblings suffer backs them into dark corners. They strike back anyway they can. They kill their own because the guilty party has fled the scene and someone must pay a price for their misery. Too many negative ingredients have stirred their pot of destruction. We feed them poison and they consume what's leftover of the leftovers. Eat enough dirt and it will seep through your pores and infect everyone around you. Turn that shit around, feed the soul righteously and stir it with hope, and we can fix some of

39

those broken pieces scattered along the curbs of our hearts.

•

The safety and well being of your son or daughter is not an American priority. There is no room for POOR CHILDREN BEING MURDERED on the political agenda. Poor children dying as a platform doesn't win elections, unless we make it a priority, *because if you would have raised your children right in the first place they wouldn't be exposed to murder and mayhem.* This is the message delivered by the unconcerned. Indifference seems the extent of their regard for human life, until it personally effects them. Truth crushed to earth always rises to the surface of the public sphere. Poverty's truth will rise, and we will all feel the bombs exploding in beautiful and wretched places. Once trauma strikes from behind ghetto walls and impacts the mainstream, they will care then. Bloodshed will spill like mortar solidifying the ugly truth which freedom often reveals. This will be both a great and tragic day, because America's greatest victories were born from tragic means. Change isn't always beautiful; it is much more than a word or idea used for political advancement. If America was to grow into a great nation, the Native American had to be annihilated. That was change. For commerce to prosper slaves were brought to America as property, used as tools for free labor, and dehumanized. That was change. Our bodies and souls have been imprisoned from the very beginning, and generations of young black men have paid the price. This, too, was change. Pain is the vessel through which real change must travel. We have endured our portion. We've inhaled deeply and sucked that shit up; now it threatens to spill from the rim of our broken hearts. At some point, it will punish the *RIGHT* side of town.

•

The poor haven't banded together because there has been no safe space to do so; no powerful place where those facing similar adversity can share ideas of what worked in solving

40

similar problems in their communities. What happened once they organized? Once they positioned themselves to take a closer look at their problems, what were the dynamics of change that took place? What happened when they looked through a different lens, one filtered with images of the human condition instead of lies delivered by a polluted political system? The media portrays our children as murderous monsters. If we were to take a closer look, these "so-called" hoodlums might become human beings again.

•

Once they have been humanized maybe we'll realize they are still *"our"* children, and they've landed on street corners from no fault of their own. Looking through a lens of clarity, maybe we'll understand why they cluster in dangerous places. The love they seek has been offered by the streets. If love is all it takes to rescue our children from self destruction why haven't we offered it? Perhaps there has been no vessel through which genuine concern can flow. We don't have the resources to lure them back from the streets. More importantly, we don't have a plan. Hugs and kisses aren't enough to reverse the damage done to these young souls. *I love you my darling* are just words if there is no foundation to solidify them; no parental or community responsibility making sure the beaten path isn't bloodied and closed off from humanity. If given ample inspiration and resources these kids can paint new lives for themselves. How? Put them to work. Educate them in ways that have never happened in America's educational system. Educators must flip the present format and look at unexplored methods of teaching that haven't been unveiled to the masses; tools that exist outside the box: tools the mainstream has chosen to ignore.

•

ALICIA, fifteen, approaches BEN standing at a bus stop. BEN is taken aback by her presence. His posture stiffens.

ALICIA
(barely glancing at him)
I didn't know you caught this bus.

BEN
I ... I just started last week.

ALICIA
Why? Didn't your mama use to pick you up from school?

BEN
Yeah. But her car broke down. So I have to take the bus.

ALICIA
That's messed up.

BEN
Yea. I guess.

ALICIA
I saw when you ask that question in class today. I think that's
the first time I ever heard you say anything in class.

BEN
(smiling a little)
I didn't know you was lookin' at me.

ALICIA
(defensive)
You wish.
(turning away slightly)
What'n nobody lookin' at you boy.

BEN
(stealing a look at her, then turning away)
I didn't know you caught the bus. I thought you lived around
here.

ALICIA
I use to. My mama died and my daddy went to jail, so I had to
move in with my Ainty.

BEN
(sympathetic)
Your mama died?

ALICIA
(barely moved)
Yea. Three months ago.
(pause)
She died.

BEN
I'm so sorry.

ALICIA
That's okay. She wasn't a good mama no way. She was more
like a cousin or a sister because she was so young when she had
me. She what'n but sixteen.

BEN
Sixteen?

ALICIA
Yea. That's too young. Even I know that's too young and she
my own mama. I was tellin' my friend that I was gonna wait
until I was at least eighteen before havin' a baby.

BEN

That's still real young.

ALICIA

Yea. But it aint nothin' like sixteen. Sixteen is way too young to be havin'a baby. I know it's okay to have sex at sixteen, and sometime even fifteen, but havin' a baby at that young age aint no good.
  (reflective)
For me, it was like I never really even had a mama.

A single gunshot rings out and ALICIA falls to the ground.
BEN is stunned. He stumbles backward and unleashes a scream.

BEN

AAAHHHHHHHHHHHH!!!!
  •
Our youth will lead this new discourse in recovery. Their insight and passion will take us the distance. They are the ones with fire and ambition. While the rest of us sit on our hands praying that Jesus will come and save us, they are living in a time of "revolution." They're the ones killing each other in the streets and fighting for their existence the only way they can. We are the ones standing in the shadows of our past, content reflecting on the Civil Rights Movement and Dr. King instead of getting our hands dirty and fighting battles worthy of our best efforts. The blood a mother wipes on our shirts is evidence that someone is out here fighting. Get in it! Revolutionize the process instead of watching from the sidelines. Each child is everyone's responsibility. Talk to them and find out what's really on their minds. Ask them what they want then show them how to get it. That's what movement means. Sometimes you have to move others before you can get moving yourself. Movement breeds momentum; momentum creates revolution.

44

We've lacked the courage to look them in the eye so we judge our youth from a distance. Trusting them with our future seems like a self-defeating prophecy. Many of us feel they've gotten it all wrong. What if we're wrong and they're right? What if our opposition to this youth culture is misplaced and we are the ones standing in the way of progress? Are we so stubborn that we can't get out of our own way? Are we so comfortable in our oppression that we refuse to give this youth movement a chance to lead? If you've given up then get out of the way and let those who are ready to fight take the reins of our future. Pass the baton so they can lead. Give them an opportunity to succeed or fail instead of dying for nothing, rendering their lives useless. Their precious lives are not useless. They were put on this earth to do great things, if we would just pry open that door to salvation and point them in
the right direction. They might screw it up; they might stumble and fall, but they will lead. We must trust them. We must follow them, or get left behind.

Republicans Hate Poor People

Lets get one fact straight. Republicans don't give a damn about poor people! They don't care about your daily struggles, and that you can't find a job or pay your rent. If your lights get shut off - your heat in the dead of winter - they blame you. Some might pretend to care. They don't, because there is no evidence. If there is no evidence THEN IT AINT TRUE! Just more lies stacked on top of the bullshit left behind by Reagan and Bush in strengthening ghetto walls. Repetition sells lies as if they were truth; say the same thing repeatedly and some folks will believe it. A handful of Americans believe Republicans because there has been no substantive opposition, and a lie beats silence any day of the week.

•

The Tea Party has made more noise over the last few years than any political movement in recent history. In spite mainstream opinion, they have proven their political worth. Dismissing them as a bunch of white people mad because the President is black would be naïve. They've forced their way into positions of power. They are moving and shaping America's political structure.

The majority of Tea Partiers are probably poor themselves, but their ideals have wandered far off the beaten path. They supposedly support tax breaks for billionaires. They carry racist signs of President Obama looking like a monkey, a buffoon and Adolph Hitler; Birthers like Donald Trump say he isn't an American. They call him a communist and a socialist. Take a closer look. They aren't just disrespecting the President of the United States, they're talking about you too. When they call for less government they're protesting against your welfare check, your food stamps, your Medicare, Medicaid and your housing subsidy. Republicans refer to the Barrack Obama as the "food stamp" President, as if helping those who have so little is a criminal offense. They are unscrupulous in their methods of destruction. If we don't get involved and recognize

46

that both recovery and redemption are needed to win this fight, we will be wiped off the face of the earth.

•

When our food stamps get cut by ten dollars we fight tooth and nail to get that amount raised, but when Republicans call for less government we are too politically "dumb down" to realize they're talking about us, the poor and disenfranchised. Yes. You! If you get cash and food stamps from the government Republicans want to take that away from you; smaller government means less for you, not them. They think you're shiftless, lazy and freeloading off the government. They believe you'd rather sit at home smoking weed and drinking a forty instead of working a job, and you're somehow content living unemployed, impoverished, and watching your dignity slip steadily through your fingers. Instead of giving you a job, Republicans want to strip you of the meager means you depend on for survival each month. You're already surviving well below the poverty line. They want to push you off the edge. You're letting them.

•

Lies or no lies, Tea Party Republicans are fighting and winning. Granted, they have flourished because of hundreds of millions of dollars contributed by billionaires like Karl Rove and the Koch brothers, who bankroll their extreme protest and political campaigns. I will give them this much; at least they have the courage to fight. Tea Party candidates have won elections; they've taken seats in Congress and the Senate. They've positioned themselves to pass legislation that is certain to take money out of your pocket. Less government means less for you! Deregulation of Wall Street and tax breaks for billion dollar corporations means that noose around your neck will only get tighter. The problem? We know the noose around our neck is tight. When those pennies, nickels and dimes don't add up we feel it choking us everyday. We know we're being

47

crushed each time we get a bill we can't pay, or when we can't provide for the basic needs of our family. When there's less food in the fridge being poor resonates like a punch to the heart. That's when poverty seeps permanently into our core.

The problem, for poor people? We've failed to identify an "enemy." Our oppressor's face is plastered on the evening news seven nights a week, but we've been so severely blinded by poverty we can't see them. Five years after electing America's first Black President we still singin' *"Oh, Happy Day"* while there are factions working diligently to push your poor behind off the edge of the earth. Being at the bottom isn't enough; they want you obliterated. *Gone!* Your presence, colored in destitution, homelessness, and painted with the blood of violence has become a stain on that beautiful portrait so many Americans like to paint of themselves. You've seen that Norman Rockwell painting where all the white people are seated in the front; blacks, Hispanics, poor, homeless, addicted, incarcerated and the mentally ill are so far in the background you can't even see them. The rich, white people are in color while everyone else is vague, abstract, and barely woven into the scenery. Republicans want you air brushed out of that painting. Your dreams don't equal their dreams. Your pain doesn't equal their pain. The lives of your children aren't as precious as their sons and daughters. Inequality is the only space available for America's poor; it is a tight space with little room to maneuver, or to find respite from unrelenting oppression. Bullets penetrate the flesh of this space, and exit wounds end the lives of our children. In an instant, sometimes even in broad daylight ... another child is just gone. This is unacceptable!

•

The Republicans are trying to play you for a fool! We must take them to task for governing via the delusional pathway. You can't ask Republicans to do the right thing; if you wait on them to have a change of heart you might as well start digging your own grave now. We must force them to do the right thing! When they scream for smaller government we must yell back for bigger government! Cries for smaller government only grew into angry mobs once a black man was elected President; this speaks of racism at it's most primitive level. If they didn't cry foul when George Bush was running America into the ground they need to shut the fuck up and do the right thing in 2014 - and beyond! Poor people don't care about their crocodile tears; we have real tears from real pain. Poor people care about what's right and wrong; what's fair and just. Republicans are a bunch of pimps. They care about money, even if it means selling America's soul in the process.

Revolution

Revolutions must be a transformation into something. Revolutionaries are programmatic in nature: they are ideological, in that they are underpinned by a specific framework or scheme of ideas; and utopian, in the sense that they hold out for the prospect of a better future.

Ben Dupree

The availability of rocks and blows as temporary relief are offered to the broken hearted, crushing them into fragments much too damaged for a one-dimensional fix. In the hood twenty-four hour liquor stores are on every other street corner, and the dope man is always nearby. Poverty lives in plain sight, but those in a position to create change refuse to make even the slightest gesture toward humanity. Money and politics have blinded them to the people's plight; a lack of resistance by poor people has lulled them to sleep. They believe sleeping giants should not be awakened, as if our pain would never spill outside the hood and we would keep burning our communities without it ever exploding into the mainstream. We own a handful of businesses, so we burn their businesses as if they were our own, out of madness and frustration.

Elements of revolution have trickled down through the generations. Humiliation, degradation and dislocation simmer like a nuclear bomb just waiting to blow. In the sixties and seventies we burned and looted local businesses because we just couldn't take it anymore. Multiply those frustrations to the tenth power and you'll see why the shit is about to hit the fan in 2014, and beyond. A combustible, historical moment inches closer as power brokers ignore America's poor. If something doesn't change soon, if someone or something doesn't pay a price or put a down payment on a solution to this misery, we will explode; our insides will splatter onto the walls of "so-called" innocent bystanders and our pain will be presented in real time. Yes, we burned our own communities in the sixties and seventies; we looted and robbed because freedom was never offered with any measure of sincerity. Generations have been told that humanity will soon land on the doorstep of our hearts. Leave your heart light on they say, it will be coming around any day now. Each generation has heard the same lie. Hope is nowhere on the horizon.

•

50

Now it has spilled. Bloodshed from an inner-city revolution has reached the elite; as if our rage would stay hidden behind ghetto walls without others paying a price, and ours would be the only blood spilled from a thus far "undocumented" revolution. The blood of the presumed innocent has splashed onto the evening news. Of course, mainstream America is only presumed innocent; black people know a serious debt remains and it needs to be paid in full. Slavery was no accident. It was born from evil and greed and no one is let off the hook when so many generations have been destroyed in its aftermath. Once we get our shit together, we will calculate that amount with interest. And we will demand full payment!

•

The audacity of one human being believing they should own another human being was the first brick laid in cementing ghetto walls. Cultures and races have finally mixed, but the recipe isn't quite right because it has been stirred in unequal portions. See those reddish, black blotches lining inner city sidewalks? That's the blood of Black and Hispanic children spilling daily into America's emergency rooms. Hear that slow, thumping sound off in the distance? That's the sound of our children's heart's beating slower and slower, until death grabs them and takes them home. Hear that woman screaming, that man cursing and those gunshots popping off in the distance? That is the pain that poverty has produced.

•

It is shameful that bloodshed is something that must now be measured. There was a time when this was unimaginable, but that time has long since passed; withered and worn by America's political agenda. Each generation is expected to surpass the next, but in the hood the cycle of life is in a constant state of disruption. Our youth generation has been sliced in half, or in the case of so many seven and eight year olds who have been murdered in the streets, into quarters: all sacrificed in the

51

name of poverty. The beautiful, hopeful light those children brought to this world has been quashed. Their absence has made the world a much darker place. We grieve for those children whose lives have been tragically cut short. Yes, we grieve, but we owe them much more than our grief; we owe them nothing less than our dreams. Their mortality is broadcast on the evening news with normalcy, as if Black and Hispanic children are expected to die violent deaths. They are fulfilling these expectations. Yes, America has taught us how to put a gun to our own head. She has taught us how to pull the trigger, but the populous is no longer immune from the repercussions of poverty spilling into the mainstream.

•

Bad blood remains. It mixes together in spite of our differences. The media has labeled this peculiar residue of revolution "Flash Mobs" or "Knock Out Artist"; clusters of black teenagers have attacked white people in downtown Chicago and in other cities across the nation. These attacks are fast and furious. Police Chiefs and Mayors say they will get a handle on things. These kids are considered hoodlums and thugs. They might be, but those spewing vile stereotypes are usually more guilty than the ones committing crimes. These attacks can't be condoned, but the river of revolution has a flow which respects neither rhyme nor reason. Its flow is reckless and tainted with inequality. Its waves are powerful and destructive, reflecting you and I and all the pain that falls in between. It will not, and cannot, be contained.

•

We, the poor, must create our own *State of Emergency*. Take a closer look at your surroundings; hope is nowhere on the scene. Don't buy that political speak suggesting times are hard on everyone because they aren't. Republicans who support tax breaks for billionaires aren't suffering. Some folks are uncomfortable, but the masses of poor people live daily, impoverished lives. Rock bottom simmers like coal burning hot against our souls, but we keep keepin on anyhow. Experts say recovery begins when a person hits rock bottom. It's getting crowded down here with so many of us crawling around on our hands and knees, picking up crumbs as if it were manna falling from heaven. It is not manna; it is bullshit thrown at you like garbage, as if you have no choice but to accept whatever is offered you.

•

It only takes a few of us to stand and try and walk again. Granted, standing on such a shaky foundation is risky; our souls are weak, and we'd prefer the structure be solid, or at least not so unsteady when taking on such a monumental task. That first step toward recovery will be the hardest some of us have taken in many years. You still have your pride ... Right? In your heart of hearts you know you should have learned to walk years ago. The flip side? It's always safer to keep crawling and accepting whatever is offered you. Fighting for change is hard work; this was omitted while hope and change toyed with our hearts in 2008. Idealism was put out there, it was beautiful and many of us took the bait. Why wouldn't we? Poor people have longed for some semblance of hope and change for more years than we can remember. In 2008 it was presented to us on a silver platter, but we forgot to read the fine print at the bottom of the menu. The President said he needed our help for America to reach her potential. Maybe he had foreseen this illogical wave of Republican resistance his first day in office. Regardless of circumstance, he has not delivered the relief he promised. We, the people, have delivered even less. If we are to survive this madness - if more of us are going to come out alive than dead, we must deliver our portion. If you decide to stand there are no guarantees you won't fall again; perhaps even harder than before. Life offers no guarantees.

•

53

Today I have decided to stand and fight! My foundation is shaky but it will never be strengthened as long as I'm lying down and allowing elitist to walk all over me. I might fall, maybe even ten or twenty times; that doesn't matter. As long as I keep getting up, moving forward and fighting against the strategic termination of poor people, I will force hope and change into my personal equation. Watch me as I walk down the street; watch me get stronger. That swagger isn't because I think I'm cool, it's because I'm confident in my ability to help change the world. I ask that you stand with me, and I will hold your hand until you're strong. If your neighbor stumbles and falls maybe you'll be there to lift them from the bottom, and you'll hold their hand. Then grandma might stand, and mama, and Junior might straighten his back up when he gets out of jail instead of going right back to the corner. And he might help his father stand, leaving that crack pipe and disillusionment on the curb he's be sitting on the last three years. Standing is a measurement of pride and dignity. What have you stood for all the years of your life? What do you stand for now? We must break the chains of the generations and build a new, invigorated pipeline through the souls of our men and women.

•

The term *Uprising* fits perfectly with the times. I use it here because of its potency. Uprising means *to rise up*; lifting those from the bottom to the top, or at the very least, onto a more equal platform. The motivation behind the Civil Rights Movement was equality. One of the first seeds planted was a Black woman's refusal to give up her seat on a bus to a white man, and from that grew a movement of monumental proportions. At the time a monumental movement was needed because in the fifties and sixties poor people were dirt poor; those dirt poor people were mostly southern blacks living within that hopeless timeline between slavery and "so-called" freedom. Their worth had been calculated by America's founding fathers as "three-fifths" human being. They couldn't vote and couldn't use the same restrooms or drink from the same water fountains as white people. Black people in Georgia, Alabama, Tennessee and Mississippi rode in the backs of buses while whites rode in the front. Jim Crow prohibited blacks from eating in the same diners or sleeping in the same hotels as whites. The Civil Rights Movement was an uprising which used the strategic method of "civil disobedience" as its weapon. Back then poor people were fed up; poor, southern blacks had finally had their fill of dehumanizing tactics practiced by racist power brokers. Because of this, a revolution exploded onto the scene.

•

Talk of "revolution" or "uprising" is taboo in American culture. Being an American means we should be content with our lower class status, even if it ranks us at the very bottom. If you're Hispanic, you shouldn't care that America wants to kick you out of the country. If you're black, forget about slavery, get off of welfare and go find a job. If you suffer from mental illness just keep talking to yourself instead of letting America know how you really feel.

•

The rich and powerful fear any mention of revolution; some consider it a prelude to unnecessary violence. What they don't realize is that poverty and violence go hand in hand, and one can't exist without the other. American hunger is sustainable, but a starving people will create their own uprising. When a point of no return is reached, death and prison become viable options just to break loose from the hell they live each day. A child or husband being murdered is revolting to the human spirit; that trauma is then given back to the world the same way it was offered. When there're no jobs, hope, and no one who really cares your personal revolution spills from your soul with reckless abandon. Blood is already flowing through the streets. The problem? It is the blood of our men and children, who have finally chosen death over prison, and the mentally ill, who have felt only pain in these United States of America.

●

Why would any American want to engage in revolutionary tactics? Why would the poor ever participate in an uprising? Why would a common people protest against their miserable condition in this country? Why would the poor want to get up off their knees and fight for their salvation? Why would the mortally crippled want to learn to walk again? America claims to be the demonstration project for future democratic nations all across the world, but she has never really practiced what she's preached. The poor have always lived at the American bottom; the feet of the rich and powerful have always trampled those financially weakened by poverty. America the beautiful is what we see on post cards. The real thing is tucked neatly away behind ghetto walls.

●

Where are the front lines? Look out your window; look on Seventy-Ninth and Cottage Grove, Madison and Pulaski, or Fifty-Fifth and Halsted on Chicago's south and west sides and tell me what you see. Mayhem in plain sight is still mayhem. See those gang bangers clustered outside that convenience store on Sixty-Second and Ellis? Their presence, writhed in danger and fear, is the result of negligence on behalf of our elected officials. They were hired to be advocates and to watch our backs, but most don't even know our names; if they did they would speak of the poor in a strong, clear voice instead of spewing meaningless rhetoric that has left us deviated and uninspired. There should be passion and outrage in their voices when they fight for us. So far, we've heard mostly silence. Look out your window again so you can really see the truth and how it affects your life. Look at that woman moving down Fifty-Seventh street. You know her, you've seen her your entire life. She was a cheer leader and president of the student council in high school. She went to college and became an accountant. Now look at her; a crack addict moving so fast she'll probably slip from humanity's edge any day now. Inevitably, if something doesn't change soon, just like the rest, she will fall into death's permanent grip.

.

Revolutionary tactics from the sixties won't work fifty years later. We have to throw some flavor into the mix; throw some new ideas in the pot with the old recipes, mix it all together, and come up with a master plan that is unique and ripe with potential. Once we start thinking outside the box we will rediscover dreams that have been lying dormant inside us for years. Remember that dream you've harbored since you were a teenager? No one knows about it but you. This is your time to bring it alive. Stimulate your own ideas and start fighting for causes close to your heart; no more attaching yourself to meaningless protests that fizzle in two or three weeks. The tools for change have been provided; fight against that turmoil weighing you down. Look around, no one is fighting to preserve your rights as an American citizen. You must fight for your portion of the American dream before it is taken from you. But we must fight realistically. Yes, there are still white people who will murder us in cold blood, and our judicial system will set them free. We are no longer fighting to share lunch counters or ride on buses with white people. There are no mobs lining Bridgeport streets ready to beat us down for wandering into their community. Our most pressing problems have been turned inward. The educational system, for poor people, is broken. Jobs paying a livable wage have been dismantled, sent to other countries, and replaced with rocks and blows. When our problems are on the inside, who do we protest? Where do you march and who is held accountable when your son or nephew is on the corner working for the enemy? That child has been blinded by poverty and can't possibly understand the damage he causes his own people. If the fight takes place from within we must solve them ourselves, and stop begging others for our salvation.

•

You don't have to stand alone and you don't have to fight alone. Get six or seven of your family and friends to come and fight with you, and find solutions to your problems with those whom you share commonalities. Start fighting the good fight, it's better than fighting each other. We wonder why our children kill each other. Take a closer look; we've offered them pain instead of progress, and prison instead of a quality education that will inspire them to reach for the stars. Give them more, and watch them shine.

•

A successful campaign is measured by the people's passion; ten or twenty can start, but thousands, if not millions are needed to cross the finish line. Today's technology provides innovative ways of organizing that weren't available during the Civil Rights Movement. We no longer have to be in the same location to organize; a platform for an effective organization has been placed on the world wide stage. The intimacy of person to person camaraderie has transformed into internet team building; social networking is a force the world is still learning to reckon with. Most poor people have cell phones. Lets try something. Put down your gun and pick up your phone; examine its potential as you hold it in your hand. That gun kills innocent people, but your phone is more powerful than any weapon on earth. Use it to blast some sense into your enemy. Blow his mind into fragments, then help him pick up the pieces and rebuild America's human condition.

•

Facebook provides a vessel through which a legitimate movement can be propelled into action. Distance is no longer an issue, our problems are national problems. Organizing through social media can keep a movement focused, but still personable; filtering out egos and personalities that often block our pathway to progress. Through text messaging we can share ideas that enhance the lives of the poor. The tools for revolution are within our midst. If used properly, we can start winning for a change instead of losing so much.

.

If you have access to the Internet, if your "Bloc" is scattered across the city or in another state, use social media for your brainstorming sessions. Once your Bloc is in problem solving mode, use Twitter to communicate ideas of what's working or not working, and what amendments need adjusting to keep your mission focused. Tweeting in alliance with the Poor People's Campaign (poor persons on Twitter) will show the world how Americans solve their problems in spite of economic inequality. Gather beneath the poor people's domain (poorpeoplescampaign@yahoo/ lower case) and stay abreast of movement activities while adding your own ideas for progress to the mix. Encourage your family and friends to join the Poor People's Campaign and they will bring their thousands of friends and followers with them; your commentary will keep this movement churning like graffiti spinning arresting colors against your soul. Write what you feel, but be respectful of the mission. Explore your vocabulary while searching for a bigger and better meaning that matches the intensity of your resolve for change. Don't be afraid to tell the world how you feel. If you don't say something now no one will ever know your story. Explain your condition so Americans will understand your pain with transparency. Movement evolves backward and forward; it expands the circumference of our lives. Forward motion equals progress, and it is the only thing that will change the dynamics of your life.

.

An effective poor people's campaign will be a visual and viral sensation. No one can say they were blind sided because revolution will be exposed for the whole world to see. If America won't acknowledge us, we will get in her face and force the issue! A world stimulated by social media and text messaging will be added to thousands of marching feet and creative minds propelling the poor people's campaign forward. Footage of the poor people's campaign will become front page news delivered by you. Media has been snatched from the teeth of newspapers and traditional journalistic outlets, and placed in the hands of the people. Each time you look at your phone or open your IPad you hold the balance of American power in your hands. Examples of Tunisia, Egypt, Libya, and Occupy Wall Street have demonstrated that giving strength to the people is empowering.

With the people is where the power has landed. America will now witness her own written words being brought to fruition. She has segregated the poor from the mainstream and silenced our voices to a whisper; she has ignored our cries for salvation in the midst of persistent turmoil, now it is out of her hands. The balance of power has been given to the masses, and we can now tell our stories truthfully instead of the fiction that's been offered as truth. The dignity of this new generation will be put forth as a witness to modern day oppression. Now the history books will be written accurately instead of suppressing the painful parts laced with shame and degradation. No more blotting out the bloody genocide of the Native American and the permanent enslavement of Black and Hispanic men locked away in prisons. Because of you, American atrocities will be exposed. Truth crushed to earth will rise again. This time we will all bear witness.

•

Spliced video from organized rallies, public debates, and brainstorming sessions will be so overwhelming "You Tube" servers will explode. If the Poor People's Campaign is to go viral it is up to you and I to send it there. Technology has provided us with the tools to present our grievances in real time. Get involved! We no longer need guns and self sacrifice to fight for equality; revolution is right there in your phone. How many text messages do you send each day? How often do you tweet? How often are you on Facebook? How often do you go on *You Tube* to watch some outrageous video that your cousin told you about? Imagine these tools being used to the tenth power? Gill Scott Herron once forecasted that the *Revolution Will Not Be Televised*; a poor people's revolution will reach beyond the limits of cable and network television. The world will know of your hardship because you will show them. They won't read about your success in history books, they will watch it live, because your life will become a demonstration for progress. You will finally speak for yourself instead of others speaking for you. Share your pain and heartache with the world like water hoses and attack dogs mauling black people in the south in the sixties. Take out your phone and record the devastation you witness every single day, and show it to the world. Record the personal disaster that has devastated your life. Stop letting that inner turmoil fester; show it to the world so they will feel your pain. Your fate is in your hands. You have the ability to change things. I'm hopeful you will find the courage to try.

•

Join the Poor People's Campaign, and we will all fight together. We will show the world the shameful circumstances simmering on the American bottom. No more blurbs on the evening news or in newspapers; show them the blood of your thirteen year old daughter flowing down the sidewalk. Show them the lost generations clustered on street corners. Show the world what genocide really looks like, and how extreme hardship isn't exclusive to third world countries. Open America's backdoor so she can really see what's out there.

61

Show her the damage and ugliness hidden like a shameful scar. Don't let them off the hook; stop letting them pull the wool over your eyes. Expose the truth in real time no matter how raw and painful it is. Get up off your knees and use the tools with which you've been provided, and fight the good fight; no one else is fighting for you.

·

Let the Poor People's Campaign be your platform. Put your truth out there so everyone can see it and they will know what misery really feels like. They will learn because you show them how poor people change their lives from negative to positive. Show them how you stand up for your rights as American citizens, and how you walk with confidence instead of fear. They will see your strength, the weak will bear witness to this *"new"* you and they will learn to walk tall again, because you will have shown them a pathway to civility. Wear your dignity like a medal of honor. Expose it to the world: to our youth, who seem willing to sacrifice their lives for whatever freedom they can find, and perhaps they'll see their own dignity in your reflection ... And the beat goes on; your life's rhythm can grow into that beautiful song you've always wanted to write, and sing. America will finally see us standing together. She will see the power of sheer numbers, and how the poor should never be counted out. Once they bear witness to revolution, they will understand that you are an American too, and you deserve your portion of the American Dream; no one is delivering that dream on a silver platter. You must take it! Show them! Let them know you mean business and they won't ignore you, because you will have put the truth right in their faces. Send message after message and post picture after picture; send the evidence of revolution through your phone or text messaging or by any means necessary. Show the world what your own personal "state of emergency" looks like. If we find hope among us, we will create change for each and every person suffering at

America's bottom.

•

What is your motivation for organization? Are you sick and
tired of being sick and tired? They say misery loves company;
pair that misery with tangible solutions and you might start a
revolution. Changing the downward trajectory of our lives must
involve more than political speak spewed to the masses to win
elections. If public officials are going to lie while running for
office they might as well spit in our faces in the beginning and
get it over with. Preaching themes of change then serving their
own interest once elected is disingenuous by any measure. Spit
on me now. At least then I know where you stand.

•

Politicians in America's inner-cities need to be overthrown.
Ghetto Walls need to be torn down and the whole thing rebuilt
from the ground up: brick by brick and person by person.
Congress needs to be overthrown before it runs America into
the dirt. State officials need to be overthrown and replaced with
persons who possess common sense instead of political agendas.
If their congressional district is decimated they should be
overthrown; kick their door in with your vote and throw them
out of office! If there's more poverty outside your door than
hope, and if they haven't done anything by now chances are
they aren't going to do anything. I'm sure these congressmen,
senators and aldermen are decent citizens. You've probably
voted for them in every election. Lets put sentimentality aside
for a moment. Even if they were once members of the Black
Panther Party or the sons of famous civil rights leaders, they
are not their fathers; heroism doesn't trickle down through the
generations. Their time has come and gone. Their names are
useless to you now. Their non-action speaks louder than words.

•

The poor have been damaged by numerous afflictions. We've
grown so desensitized by poverty that pain has integrated into

63

our core. Accepting one's own decline represents backward motion. Remaining complacent while engulfed in humiliating, unacceptable living conditions means you've waved the white flag. If poor people lack empowerment, they lack the will to fight for their rights. If there's no sense of community the poor will remain fragmented and dehumanized. With no clear process for revolutionizing our lives, we have become the biggest impediment in our road to progress. We often trip over ourselves while trying to make even one positive step forward. In many respects these roadblocks are strong because we tend to go it alone. *This is my fight and I can handle it myself,* we say. But we can't. When you're weak, how can you expect to fight and win while going it alone? Put your struggle with someone else's struggle, then add a few more like minds along the way. Brainstorm your plan, then go to battle for your own salvation.

•

That teenager who avoided the corner and went to the library instead, is a revolutionary. That teacher who has been forced to think outside the box so her children can learn, she's already on the front lines fighting! That unemployed contractor who knows how to rebuild the inner-cities' crumbling infrastructure is yearning for something he can feel. That single mother with five kids who has come up with innovative ideas for using non-for-profit status in business is already walking in the future! There is gold among poor people. There are brilliant ideas lying dormant inside each of us ... If we would only start talking to each other again; not that stereotypical, meaningless crap about it being such a nice day or the cold lasting too long, but real talk that creates change. We don't have to like each other; we don't even have to be friends. We just need to talk, in someone's backyard or living room, at the library or in a coffee shop, face to face or on Facebook, Twitter or person to person, using real dialogue instead of the political speak we get from our public servants. President Obama isn't riding in on a white horse to save us. We must share our ideas, mesh them together, and learn how to solve our own problems. If we don't, many more will perish.

•

There's power in numbers; that power solidifies into millions of strong, deliberate hearts once we organize. One poor person standing alone voicing their discontent is equal to that preacher on a street corner screaming for the wicked to change their self-destructive ways. That preacher might be right, the wayward need to change, but he offers no pathway to redemption. That lone preacher offers no tools for recovery, rendering his platform baseless. One poor person standing alone is easily ignored; add one thousand standing beside him, and America will pay attention.

Free your Mind, and Recovery Will Follow

Freeing ones mind should never be taken lightly. The brain gives us our life instructions; it instructs us to use our hands, feet, and when we should smile or frown. When tragedy strikes the brain stimulates emotion, and sheds tears from our eyes. When we are overjoyed the brain creates laughter. The brain tells us to the pull that trigger when we're trying to kill a rival gang member, even when a ten year old is in the line of fire. The brain tells us to suck that dick to get that rock because that rock will instantly alleviate the pain which threatens to take us under. The brain does these things; it instructs us to put one foot in front of the other, and to fall when we are broken. No matter if they are good or bad decisions, the brain decides.

The brain is the most powerful human instrument in the world; it creates beauty and pain through avenues of freedom and oppression. What happens when the brain is damaged? Trauma deletes elements of compassion and discernment from its most intricate cavities. Being raped at age four, and seven, and again at eleven, and beaten by a stepfather and dehumanized by the media and other public officials, and terrorized, and loved by the local gangs, has a profound impact on the brain of a seventeen year old boy from the hood, When told by their mothers that "you ain't shit!" or "you no-good just like your daddy!" their hearts harden. They've remained hardened.

•

Freeing ones mind is much more than a catch phrase. Freedom determines our quality of life, or our willingness to die from the despair which hopelessness has produced. If the brain isn't sufficiently nourished it won't function properly. From no fault of their own, the truly disadvantaged suffer from severe brain damage. Cells destroyed by drugs, poverty and trauma have numbed our senses and desensitized our values. We need emergency surgery to repair the damage, so blood can once again flow freely to the soul without all the bullshit getting in the way.

•

Metaphorical brain surgery is no less intricate than physical brain surgery. The instruments used in performing such a delicate procedure are complex. Trained surgeons are in the trenches right now, moving through the streets and helping those devastated by poverty to repair their souls. These surgeons fight the good fight every single day. The problem? There are more wounded than there are revolutionaries. Those suffering the worst don't know where to find the help they desperately need.

•

Those qualified to perform metaphorical brain surgery should report to the front lines immediately, before the body count rises even higher. Outreach and mental health workers, therapists and psychologists, counselors and trauma specialists are needed now more than ever because the death toll among America's poor rises each day. Substance abuse specialists are needed to combat addiction that has ravished millions of families; Community Support Teams are needed to stabilize neighborhoods on the brink of collapse; artists, writers, poets and musicians are needed to remove guns from the hands of our children, and replace them with pens and paper, paint brushes and an assortment of yellow oils and green pastels so they can paint new lives for themselves. Replace rocks and blows with saxophones and drums that will recreate the music of the world in all its splendor, providing oxygen to a brain that has been suffocating for far too long. Replace fear with inspiration. Most of all, we must forgive those brothers who have hurt us. We must forgive them, because no one has ever offered them a pathway to redemption. They have fallen so far from when they were Kings they can no longer see a light at the end of the tunnel. We the people can be the light that guides them out of prison, and back onto the American platform.

·

Change has sputtered along. That glimmer of hope has been
stamped out; smoke from its dampened ashes simmers inside us
all. We want to do better but the road to success is blocked.
Recovery is the next step. We all need recovery. Fathers need to
recover from imprisoned lives. Mothers need to recover from
lifting a burden meant to be carried by two. Children need to
recover from the turmoil that has shaped their lives since birth.
If we could, we would snatch the bad shit from inside of them
and replace it with beauty, but it needs to be surgically
removed. Inspiration is cultivated from the inside. Something or
someone touches us, and we move. If there's too much bullshit
in the way there's no room for the good parts to grow; there's
no room for inspiration when hatred has already filled the void.

·

The truly disadvantaged don't know where recovery begins.
Where is the point of attack when the battle takes place from
within? No strategy has been developed for correcting what's
wrong in the soul. When everything is wrong and nothing is
right, when personal challenges are so daunting our growth is
stunted, where does the recovery process begin? How do we
get from point A to B when C isn't even in the picture? The
waters of our lives are murky; waves of oppression move
through us like a storm with no end in sight; just pouring down
hard and threatening to drown us in poverty. The American
Dream was built from a mold of exclusion. If you're poor, if
your complexion is black or brown, you were born to be
excluded in a nation which proclaims freedom for all. The origin
of that freedom was proven a lie hundreds of years ago. Now it
has been made plain. Those hoodlums on street corners
and standing in front of liquor stores aren't really hoodlums
at all; they are neither gang bangers nor thugs. They are the
traumatized and hopeless surviving the only way they know

how. Their courage has been siphoned over the course of many generations. Those sculpting their lives have offered only pain and an ample means of destruction. We stand by idly, and watch them implode.

●

We will recover, and rebuild our lives through strength and determination. It won't take rocket science, nor will the debilitating effects of gradualism impede our journey to recovery. We have already waited too long. Our time is right now! No need to beg and grovel for the slightest portion of humanity. The choices have been simplified, but we still must choose. Change, or die! Stand for something or fall further into poverty's abyss. Your children, my children, and future generations depend on your making the right choice.

Reclaim the Pieces of your Soul

As we stand, we will retrieve the pieces of our dignity along the way. Reach down and get it from that dirty alley where you left it, when you were down on your knees doing the devils work. Snatch it! Steal it! Con its way back into your soul if you must; it belongs to you and no one else has the right to possess it. Put it back in its proper place. Walk by that liquor store you once frequented ten times a day. You can handle it. That clean time is stacked high enough where they can't even see the old you anymore, because the new one is so fresh and so clean.

You'll begin to feel stronger once your dignity is back in place, then go and reclaim your pride. Maybe you didn't even know it was missing, sacrificed unknowingly through job loss and trauma. You didn't see it get up and walk out the door while you sat on the couch smoking your eighth rock in eight hours, or when you left it behind at four in the morning when you finally left the bar, but your pride decided to stay behind.

Reclaiming your life's armor will be hard work. We've fallen so far from the American Dream that dignity and pride seem like long, lost friends. We've missed their unity for so long we've forgotten how much joy they bring when they reunite. Rejoice as our senses fill to the brim. Don't stop the flow. Let it spill over so it can touch everyone around you.

•

Learning to walk instead of crawling stimulates movement. As our stride grows stronger and our swagger more confident, our minds eye will become microscopic, and our sightlines will expand once we stand for something worthwhile. Some might wonder why we've sacrificed the pieces of our soul without getting a better return. They can't know unless they were there; unless they've held their sixteen year olds son's lifeless body in their arms, or watched that strong black man, a father of four, a twenty-five year employee at Ford, crumble into addiction at age fifty - they can't know. They weren't there and words will never help them understand. So push on.

•

Search the drug dins, basements and garages you once
frequented, and try and find the courage you left on the streets.
Those who've claimed it won't give it back easily. Our missing
courage has forced us onto life's grand stage, standing beneath
a dim light and playing the role of helpless victim, when courage
once made us strong. Courage helped us protect our families
and work two jobs to try and make a better life for future
generations. Courage gave us the fortitude to lead by example:
going to work everyday, then to our kid's school to meet with
their teachers, and back home and seated at the head of the
dinner table, praying with our families as men. Our missing
courage is now locked away in prison, ravished by addiction, or
stuck on street corners because we have somehow found safety
in dangerous places. It may take weeks of battle to reclaim our
courage; drug dealers and pimps know it is worth more than
they'll ever get in return. There will be hard times involved in
taking it back. We'll want to give up, because crack and whisky
once filled those painful voids laced with degradation. Take a
deep breath, make the right choice, and keeping fighting.

•

Once our *courage* is reclaimed, and reintroduced to *pride* and
dignity, we will possess a lethal combination capable of
changing dire circumstances that have spun perilously out of
control. Courage is elusive; keep looking. While riding the "L"
downtown on your way to work or school, keep searching for
your courage. Try to remember where you left it. What were
you doing when you abandoned it, or it abandoned you? Have
faith that you will find it. Courage can't be killed; it can't be
murdered with a bullet or blown up by a bomb. You can't rape
or molest courage because the worst of times only makes it
stronger. Your husband can't beat the courage out of you no
matter how hard he tries. Some might trick you into believing
courage has been permanently extracted from your soul. Don't

71

be fooled. It has merely been put aside, awaiting your reclamation. You will stand. You will walk. You will become more confident as you reclaim the missing pieces of your life's armor; then you will break the chains of the generations, and build something new and powerful this world has never seen.

What is a Bloc?

A "Bloc" is a group of like-minded individuals banded together to address the needs of America's poor. Those needs can be your own or the needs of others. Maybe you run a small business, a barbershop or a small convenient store and you're struggling to stay afloat. There might be ten other businesses suffering from a similar financial hardship, but we're so disconnected in our poverty one business doesn't know the other exist. The Poor People's Campaign will provide a platform for these businesses to link and form a cohesive Bloc.

If your community is riddled with gang and drug activity, if that liquor/grocery/cell phone store a block from your home charges too much for a loaf of bread or gallon of milk, if their behavior is racist, foul and adds to the toxic climate of your community, if they allow gang members to cluster and sell drugs in and around their premises; residents who are willing to fight can form a "Bloc" and attack these issues head on. That's not happening now. We complain to each other, but our complaints quickly dissolve into disillusionment. If there's no follow up, movement comes to a screeching halt.

•

Organizing your own "Bloc" creates an individualized coalition for change. The mainstream has sucked us in, digested us, spat us out, and stripped us of our individualism. Lets get together and collect those pieces from the scattered sidewalks of our lives, arm's locked and moving to the rhythm of our own beat as we protest right from wrong. We will hold each other up until we are all strong again.

•

Blocs represents strength, organization and community development on a socio-political level. If poor people are to improve their lives, they need better options. Talk is cheap; people need something they can feel. For those struggling at the American bottom, corporeal change is the only thing that will make a difference.

•

What are some of the political advantages of incorporating as a Bloc? We are more powerful as an organized body. Scattered we are nothing, but together we form a powerful fist capable of knocking down ghetto walls. Blocs can attack injustice in real time instead of waiting on politicians, the police, or local officials to decide what's "fair" or "unfair." When we're given a parking ticket unjustly, we go to court and contest that ticket. If we think a store has overcharged us, we fight back. If our families are threatened, we defend them. If our food stamps get cut, we protest. If we feel we're being taken advantage as workers, we unionize. Fighting back is the American way. Poor people have a plethora of complaints, but no action. When we're outraged by community violence we take to the streets, we march, cry, shout and carry signs in expression of our grievance. Two weeks later, passion dissolves into cynicism, and we go home and slam the door on that "thing" that once moved us profoundly. Get into the streets and stay there. Protest like it is your second job.

•

A "Bloc" is also a group of individuals who live in the same vicinity. The *physical bloc* is powerful because its people live in the trenches. Their first and second job is survival, and they often make ends meet by hook or crook. They dodge bullets while waiting in line for a box of food, because all resources have been exhausted and "hood economics" have prevailed. Working families move out, drug addicts and dealers move in - squatting in abandoned homes and storefronts - and the block is quickly shoved to the American bottom. Like a plant suffering from malnutrition, it crumbles to the ground. These "broken blocks" can be salvaged, and strengthened. If a handful of concerned residents band together and form a cohesive unit, these fractured pieces of our community can be repaired. You don't need to confront the drug dealers, gang bangers, and

74

addicts or insist that they vacate the premises; incorporate them into the recovery process. When a sixteen year old boy, or twenty-two year old young man, or forty-five year old ex-felon gets out of prison and returns to the block, don't lock your door, welcome them to the table and offer them what they'll need to thrive; link them with counseling so they can heal from trauma corroding their souls from years of incarceration; put them to work doing something, anything that will keep them focused and inspired; show them a pathway to righteousness and they will become contributors to the community instead of detriments. They will become husbands again, and fathers, and sons, and nephews, and uncles, instead of criminals.

Brainstorming

Brainstorming is the single most potent tool of the poor people's campaign. We must help ourselves. THE GOVERNMENT IS NOT COMING TO SAVE YOU! They have neither the will nor desire to climb down that bottomless stairwell and witness the hell you live everyday. What do you do when your bills exceed your income? How do you respond when your life is on the brink? When the stress becomes too much and you wonder how much more you can bear, where do you turn? I'll tell you. You pray, fight, or die. The problem? Too many are dying and too few are fighting. Fighting to stay above water makes you resilient; focus, determination, passion, and fear become intertwined and you are propelled toward tangible solutions. When you're backed into a corner and there's no room to maneuver, you go to war; you fight until you've exhausted every possible avenue in solving your problem. No stone is left unturned. When you're down in the trenches fighting for your life no idea is unworthy of exploration. You push and press, you cajole and agitate; sometimes you lie and cheat because all is fair in war. While scraping and scuffling to keep from falling from life's jagged edge, you do what is necessary to survive. You attack your problem from every angle. You brainstorm your problem until it is resolved, or at the very least, until all possibilities have been exhausted.

•

Fighting the good fight is exhausting. Like scoring a winning touchdown or the winning basket, you're tired once you've fought your way to the goal line. It's time we start winning more than we lose. Fighting won't cost you a dime, and the payoff will prove worthy of your best efforts. Winning makes it all worthwhile. Winning inspires. Winning makes you stronger and more confident. Each small victory becomes a personal miracle, and once that beat catches a groove little things become life changing events. Change is within our midst, but we must sacrifice something to get something beautiful in return.

•

Brainstorming. We do it subconsciously each day. We brainstorm our problems while riding the train to work or while driving in our cars during rush hour. We replay that "thing" causing us so much trouble and wonder how it blew so far out of proportion? How did "this" become so problematic? Is that lowdown man or no good woman weighing you down? Or is the repo man hounding you and threatening to come and snatch your car? How do you scrape up that fifteen hundred dollars to keep "the man" from crawlin' up your back and choking you from behind? Or how do you get that low down mug out of your house so he won't come back no more? Hope of seminal solutions dash through our minds like an eight millimeter movie. We pause, rewind, and fast forward our collected struggles; we dissect that "thing" down to the bone. These battles are won and lost. With a little effort and dedication, we can start stacking more wins than losses.

•

We think of our problems as being exclusive, and we debate them in isolation. There are hundreds, if not thousands of others out there with similar problems. Imagine brainstorming your problem with five or ten people. Sharing ideas allows solutions to unfold instinctively, because you will have widened your spectrum of concern; the likelihood of discovering answers to your problem then heightens. Others will contribute solutions to problems that may have eluded us while confined in our self-imposed isolation. Brainstorming generates a sense of freedom. Holding freedom in your hands is liberating, and liberation strengthens the weaponry needed to tear down ghetto walls. Watch them as they crumble; wave goodbye as they dissipate before your very eyes. Release the heartache that's held you captive for so many years, and we will begin to rebuild our neighborhoods, and retake ownership of our lives and communities.

•

Brainstorming. The concept sounds wild, and it is. Putting "brain" with "storm" is combustible, and it should be. Some of us need to blow the bullshit from our lives and rebuild from the ground up. Lets get together and figure this thing out instead of depending on those who've proven they don't give a damn. I'm talking Republicans and Democrats, because neither democracy nor a republic exist in the lives of America's poor. "We The People." That's us. We can only be excluded from the American equation if we remain weak and vulnerable. If those in power won't invite us into the political discussion, we will start our own conversation, and solve our own problems.

•

Brainstorming and organizing go hand in hand; each maximizes our potential. Once ideas are formulated we need a place to collect them, decipher them, enhance them, and throw those ideas into the universe and see if they work. Everyone has ideas, but we rarely use them to our advantage. Some of us have extraordinary ideas for bettering the lives of our families, but we lack the organizational skills to hold it all together. The result is chaos; great ideas have gone awry. Selling that rock sounded like a good idea; it stacked that paper for a minute but quickly disintegrated into thirty to life, or worse, sudden death. Some of us have brilliant ideas on how to better our communities, but we lack a plan of action. Our ideas are then placed in the category of "random thought," and dissolve into nothing. We often die before seeing our ideas through to fruition. You have to do the work and put all the necessary pieces together, or you'll never know what your dreams really look like. They may not be all that pretty in the beginning, but don't give up. Sometimes you have to tweak your dreams to make them as beautiful and powerful as you've always imagined they might be.

78

•

Brainstorming is a procedure for groups and individuals to develop ideas and problem solve. We barter and compromise with "ourselves" and "others" each day; which bills can be paid on Thursday and which ones can wait until next week? When can I write a check to cover the light, gas, and water bill so they won't get shut off, hoping and praying that check doesn't hit the bank before Friday's direct deposit? Over the last few years our purchasing power has been drastically reduced; that's when that difficult decision hits you. Should you go to the food pantry and stand in a line two blocks long for a box of food, or starve while clinging to your pride? In the midst of your personal poverty you figure out when or if you can buy your kids new clothes? When can you get your car fixed? And when you have no other choice but to resort to "hood economics."

America has forced many of us to the "unrighteous" side of town; we haven't gone their willingly. Flipping loose squares, socks and chews, and dubs of weed become viable means of survival when there are so few economic opportunities available. You do what you must to take care of your babies. Through brainstorming, we can discover a better way of living without pawning our dignity in the process.

•

Brainstorming is a tangible way of solving a variety of issues concerning the poor. Inner-cities dynamics are a hotbed for revolution. The politics of the poor, addicted, jailed and imprisoned, chronic homelessness, and those suffering from poor mental health are currently absent from America's table of plenty. We need to bring a big bowl of our own shit and put it on the table right next to theirs. Our dish might have a different flavor, but it is still food for thought. And it needs to be in the mix.

•

79

Any topic can be explored through Brainstorming, especially controversial topics:

What can be done to bring jobs back to our communities?

How do we stop the senseless murder and mayhem in our inner-cities?

How can I rid my block of drug dealers clustered on street corners?

How can my Bloc use green life methods to enhance economic opportunity and clean up neglected neighborhoods?

•

Don't wait! Just do it! If you let it simmer too long you'll talk yourself out of it. Think about your most pressing problem, then think of two or three people you know who have similar problems. Now you have a "Bloc." It's that simple. Become a friend of the poor people's campaign. Present your problem or idea, set up a time for a brainstorming session, and let us guide you through the process. If you have access to the internet it won't cost you a dime. If you have the courage to fight, inspirational solutions will be your reward.

•

The *team leader* is the head of your Bloc. "He" or "She" will provide the passion and determination to help guide your Bloc toward solutions. The team leader quashes skepticism, and is responsible for keeping your Bloc fired up to do the hard work necessary to create change. The team leader keeps your Bloc focused on a single project instead of wandering in various directions. He or she inspires us to keep trying the ideas we've brainstormed, and to give them a chance to work. Your Bloc is a regiment in an army built to fight poverty and all its influential agents. When we are attacked with different afflictions and a barrage of hard times are flung at us from ghetto walls, we want solutions. Those solutions are currently unavailable. Your Bloc will make them attainable. If you get stuck, combine your ideas to create a more tangible plan to solve your problem. Circumstances might be dire, but the team leader encourages you to keep fighting; keep pushing and prodding against ghetto walls until they collapse. The team leader is courageous, and his or her passion should be contagious. Let them infect you. Embrace the team building process; let that passion overflow, and spill out into the world.

•

The *"team leader"* is also the "facilitator" of the brainstorming session: The trick is to create the right structure for the process to work, but don't over control it. Here are some of the traditional steps in the brainstorming procedure.

1. Preparation

Give your Bloc a broader landscape and decide on the brainstorming "issue" in advance. This gives Bloc members ample opportunity to stew over the possibilities. Subconsciously, we ruminate over thousands of possibilities each day. Brainstorming combines your ideas with the ideas of others, narrows them down to the three best strategies for implementation, and gets busy transforming those ideas into action.

2. Fact-Finding

Take a close look at the problem you're trying to solve. Dissect it quietly and individually; silence among peers stimulates ideas. Souls are often stirred through silence and prayer. Meditation collects our ideas and filters them through our core.

Start off by clearly defining the problem, idea, or issue to be "solved." Write the proposed question on a legal pad or chalk board. Discuss the specifics of the problem or idea so your Bloc clearly understands your goal.

4. Idea-Finding

This is where the actual brainstorming begins. All ideas and suggestions should be put on the table.

Don't judge, ridicule, or in anyway criticize anything anyone says. Like a meaningful song, don't interrupt the creative flow.

DON'T HOLD BACK! Say whatever is on your mind. Anything goes. The wilder the idea, the better. Let your imaginations flow freely. Fanatical ideas stimulate useful ones. Transform those ideas into tangible solutions.

Brainstorm until the well runs dry. Sort through your ideas, and pick a few that can immediately be put into play.

Combine, change, improve, add to, modify, improve on other people's ideas. Can another idea be adapted, magnified, minimized, substituted, rearranged, reversed, combined?

The Brainstorming session should be loose and freewheeling, which is an important part of the team building process.

Remember, nothing is set in stone until the session is complete.

5. Solution-Finding

This is where your ideas are examined and evaluated. What "ideas" or "solutions" might be most effective? Are some too simple or complex? What is practical/feasible and what isn't? What are the potential results and consequences once these ideas are put into play? Narrow your list down by a process of elimination.

6. Implementation

Try them out and see if they work. Measure your progress over the days, weeks, and months of implementation. If progress becomes stagnant, use other ideas stimulated from your brainstorming session. If necessary, reunite with your Bloc and brainstorm again. Brainstorming is a continuum. If the scale of a problem is complex, multiple brainstorming sessions might be needed before seeing results. We want results, not rhetoric. The only way to make that happen is to keep pushing and fighting until the problem is solved or your idea has blossomed. Fight through the brainstorming process as if your life depends on it, because it might. The war against poor people has been one-sided for far too long. It needs to be revolutionized. The weapons for progression are in your hands. Use them!

www.ingramcontent.com/pod-product-compliance
Lightning Source LLC
Chambersburg PA
CBHW060432290526
45791CB00002B/929

* 9 7 8 1 4 9 4 8 4 1 9 2 8 *